ISBN: 978-1727131536

A GUIDE TO
HUMANS

LAURENCE THOMAS

Here we are, Zobb!
What's this?
This is a small, watery planet called Earth. We're here to learn about a rather strange species called humans. Come along, we've a lot to get through!
Can we have lunch first?
There will be plenty of food to try when we get there. Hurry!

PLANET EARTH

The Earth is 4.5 billion years old. Humans have only been on the planet around 300,000 years, but they've made a lot of changes. So, what are these odd, two-legged creatures we call 'humans?'

WHAT IS A HUMAN?

A human is an animal, related to all other animals on Earth, and very closely related to apes, such as chimpanzees and gorillas. They have many basic similarities with apes, but many differences too.

NOPE!

YES!

ALSO NOPE!

The human species is also called 'Homo Sapiens', which is Latin for 'Wise man'.

WISE STUFF

They are the only living species under the genus 'Homo' - other relatives such as Homo Erectus and Neanderthals have been extinct for thousands of years.

Humans live like many other animals. They can:

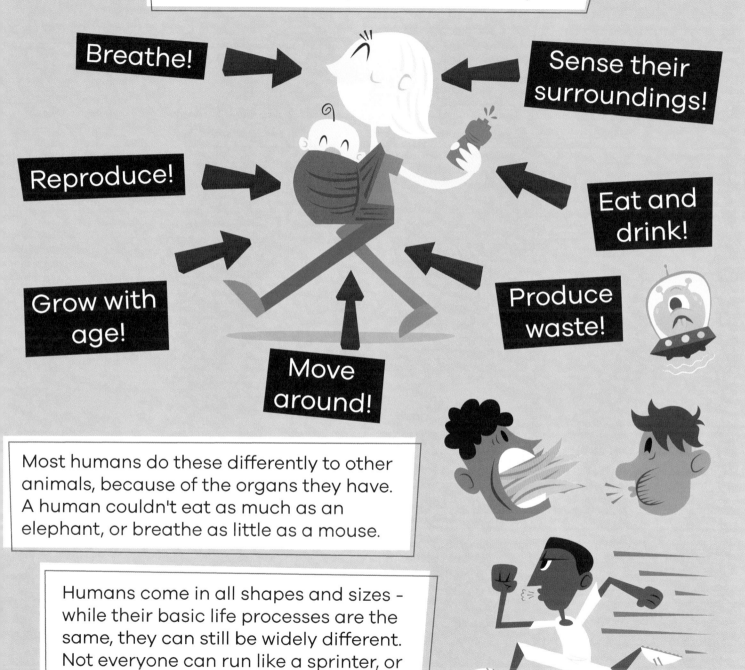

Breathe!

Sense their surroundings!

Reproduce!

Eat and drink!

Grow with age!

Produce waste!

Move around!

Most humans do these differently to other animals, because of the organs they have. A human couldn't eat as much as an elephant, or breathe as little as a mouse.

Humans come in all shapes and sizes - while their basic life processes are the same, they can still be widely different. Not everyone can run like a sprinter, or grow six feet tall - they're all unique!

Humans, and all other animals and plants, contain DNA - a collection of molecules that contain genes.

Genes have instructions that allow physical features to be passed down from their parents, such as...

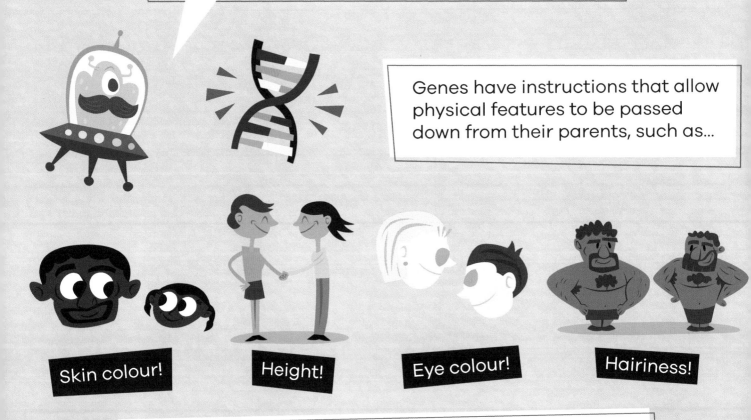

Skin colour!

Height!

Eye colour!

Hairiness!

A human's personality comes from their genes, too - but it's also affected by what they do and who they meet.

WORLD HISTORY

EPIC NOVEL

SCIENCE N' STUFF

Humans are not apes, but they do share a common ancestor who lived several million years ago. This may sound like a long time, but they still share 96% of their DNA with chimps.

They also share 90% of their DNA with a cat, and 60% with a banana!

Animals and plants are all connected in a 'tree of life'. Horses, chickens, sharks, sunflowers...

Umm... I thought we were learning about humans?

...oh yes, that's right. Ok, let's continue!

WHAT DO THEY LOOK LIKE?

Humans may have very similar genes, but they often look quite different to each other. There is a wide range of skin colours which come from changes over thousands of years, including different cultures mixing with others.

Humans from countries like Brazil have a wide mix of people who originate from Europe, Africa, Asia and elsewhere, which creates an incredible variety of skin colours within one nation.

This is happening more and more over the world, giving them a better understanding of people of different colours.

They can also look different based on other factors, such as gender and age.

Physical differences such as these have caused problems throughout history, and many have fought for their rights to be treated as equal.

Humans also like to change their appearance based on trends, culture or simply what they enjoy. This includes...

Fashion!

Makeup!

Hairstyles!

HELLO!

Tattoos!

All humans are equal. Sure, they may look quite different, but it's these differences that make them so fascinating.

WHERE DO THEY LIVE?

All over the world!... well, mostly. 70% of the Earth is covered in water, so humans mainly stick to the land.

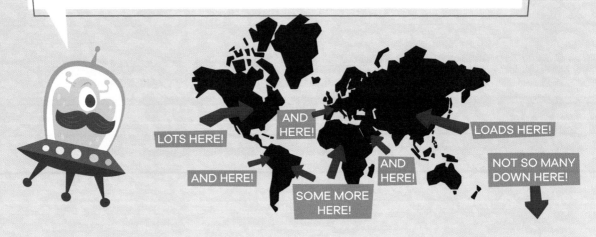

LOTS HERE!

AND HERE!

AND HERE!

SOME MORE HERE!

AND HERE!

LOADS HERE!

NOT SO MANY DOWN HERE!

Some areas can be dangerous to humans if they are incredibly hot or cold, but there are still small communities that live in them...

The Bedouin people travel across the scorching deserts of North Africa and the Middle East.

 The Inuit make their homes in the freezing Arctic regions of North Canada and Greenland.

Over 60% of humans live in the continent of Asia. That's a whole lot compared to Oceania, which has only a tiny 0.5%!

There are many types of buildings which people live in, including flats, houses, cabins, cottages...

Even castles! (although not many humans live in them nowadays...)

There are also many types of settlement for humans, from tiny villages, to towns, to huge megacities. Tokyo, the capital city of Japan, has over 38 million people in its metro area - that's a bigger population than most countries!

WHICH LANGUAGES DO THEY SPEAK?

Loads of them! There are thousands of languages in the world, many of which have millions of speakers. The most spoken language of all is Mandarin with over 1.2 BILLION speakers.

The top ten languages by the number of speakers are...

 Mandarin — Hindi

¡Hola!

 Spanish — English

 Arabic — Portuguese

 Bengali — Russian

Guten Tag!

 Japanese — German

 Some languages have more speakers outside their original countries than inside! For example, Portuguese is from Portugal, but has over 200 million speakers in Brazil.

A large number of languages are only spoken by small villages and tribes. This means that many languages have gone extinct in past centuries as other languages have taken over.

Many humans are multilingual, meaning they speak more than one language...

The only official language of France is French, but many French citizens can speak a language from a nearby country, such as English or German.

Most people from Luxembourg know FOUR languages (Luxembourgish, French, German and English)!

The USA has Spanish as its second most spoken language. Although they mostly speak English, the USA has no official language.

Zimbabwe has 16 official languages! The most widely spoken language is Shona.

HOW DO THEY STAY HEALTHY?

Humans drink water, and 60% of their body is made of it! They also need food to survive, but to stay happy and healthy they need a variety of it from different food groups, to get nutrients such as vitamins, protein and carbohydrates.

Kale is very high in vitamin K, which keeps the heart healthy.

Salmon has lots of omega-3, which improves mental health.

Almonds contain protein, which helps lower cholesterol.

Food and water is essential for human growth, energy and life itself - a human can only survive one week without water. Yikes!

Humans also need exercise to keep fit. It helps them...

Build muscle!

Lose weight!

Be happy!

Fight off diseases!

Relax better!

Common exercises include running, cycling and weight-lifting. Sports such as football, tennis and cricket are also a great way of exercising within a team. There are other fun methods too, like yoga and dance classes - getting groovy helps you stay healthy!

In fact, relaxation is just as important! All humans need sleep to survive - not too much, not too little. Just like exercise, it helps their bodies and minds stay healthy, especially when it is kept regular.

WHAT DO THEY DO FOR FUN?

When it comes to having fun, every human is different. Some love to be outside and active, while others prefer to relax indoors. Here are just some of the ways humans enjoy life (recognise some of these from earlier?)

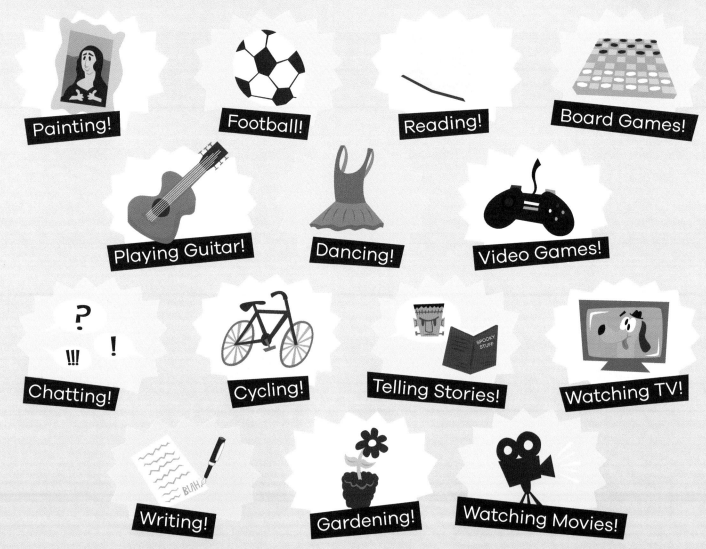

Painting!

Football!

Reading!

Board Games!

Playing Guitar!

Dancing!

Video Games!

Chatting!

Cycling!

Telling Stories!

Watching TV!

Writing!

Gardening!

Watching Movies!

Many of these are a form of art. Art is when humans create something using just tools and their imagination, to entertain themselves and others with its beauty.

Normally humans think of art as paintings and sculptures, but it can also mean writing poetry, planting flowers and even making catchy pop songs (and dancing to them)!

Just like other animals, humans love playing, which means doing an activity just for fun. To enjoy life, humans need a healthy balance of...

...and...

HOW ARE THEY CONNECTED?

Humans are all related to each other through their ancestors, but they also have smaller groups of relatives called families. This is normally a group of parents or guardians and their children. There are also extended families, which includes grandparents, aunts, uncles, cousins and many more!

Humans are also connected through friendships and partnerships.

It's a great way for humans to understand each other's likes, dislikes, beliefs and feelings (and of course, to have fun)!

There are other types of community in which humans are connected to each other, such as...

Villages!

Sports Teams!

School Classes!

Fan Clubs!

Businesses!

Religions!

Religions are some of the biggest communities on Earth - so let's find out a bit more about them, shall we?

WHAT DO THEY BELIEVE?

Humans have many different beliefs as to where they come from, why they are alive, and what happens afterwards. Groups with similar beliefs are called religions. Some of the biggest religions around include...

Christianity (2.4 billion)

Islam (1.8 billion)

Hinduism (1.1 billion)

Buddhism (500 million)

Folk Religions (400 million)

Although they have their differences, they can also share similar beliefs. For instance, Christians and Muslims believe in an afterlife, and that the universe has a God as its creator. Theories such as these have been discussed and questioned over thousands of years.

Many humans are spiritual, which means they believe in a human spirit or 'soul', different to the physical body but still connected to it.

They may also believe that they are connected to the planet, and even the universe, in ways science can't explain.

Although some religions have similar beliefs to this, not all spiritual humans are religious.

Philosophies such as Buddhism are considered by some to be a type of non-religious spirituality.

Many religions have prayer, a way of connecting and speaking to God in times of need or praise.

To connect with nature and the whole universe, spiritual humans like to meditate. Meditation can also be useful for keeping focus, or simply relaxing!

HOW DO THEY LEARN?

Most humans are educated at school when they are children and teenagers. Some of them are able to go into higher education, such as colleges and universities. They normally do this to gain all the knowledge and skills ready for their career.

School is full of different subjects. Humans will usually prefer one or more subjects over others. This is a good thing - humanity works because different people enjoy different areas of study, which gives them doctors, astronauts, police officers, chefs... and so much more!

Humans can learn in their everyday lives, too. Reading non-fiction books gives them more knowledge on certain subjects, like science and history. Fiction books and stories allow them to understand other people's lives - even if the characters aren't humans themselves!

However, the best way of learning is simply living! Humans learn from talking and playing with each other, and from their own achievements and mistakes. It's ok for people to make mistakes, as this is what helps them to develop.

HOW DO THEY HELP EACH OTHER?

Humanity can be tough. Many humans are unhappy, in pain, or not being treated fairly. Thankfully, a lot of this suffering can be eased with the help of others.

CHARITY

A charity is an organisation that raises money for those in need, such as those with diseases or living in poverty. Many charities run with the help of volunteers, who will work for the sake of helping others.

ACTIVISM

Activist groups aim to bring changes in society. Types of activism include writing to politicians, street marches and strikes. Many activists in the past have successfully fought against racism, sexism and other types of prejudice.

HEALTHCARE

Many lovely humans around the world work as doctors and nurses. Their aim is to help people with all types of illnesses. This means not only do they have to be very smart, but very caring too!

ONE-TO-ONE DISCUSSION

In many cases, the only thing a human needs is support from friends and family. Not only does socialising with others help with their wellbeing, but they can also discuss ways of fixing the problem.

RANDOM ACTS OF KINDNESS

Sometimes it's the little things that matter! This can be opening the door for someone, giving them a surprise gift, or even sharing a smile. Every action makes a difference.

WHO ARE SOME EXTRAORDINARY HUMANS?

Gosh, there are so many to choose from! Here's just a small selection of helpful humans who have had a huge impact on planet Earth.

Guatama Buddha
(c. 5th Century BCE, Nepal)

Travelled across South Asia to teach his learnings of inner peace and happiness, leading to the creation of Buddhism.

Socrates
(c. 470 BCE, Greece)

Invented the beginnings of modern Western philosophy, which he taught in Athens to many students.

Jesus
(c. 5BC, Judea)

Travelled thousands of miles to teach love, forgiveness and equality, leading to the creation of Christianity.

Leif Erikson
(920, Iceland)

Sailed the Atlantic ocean and discovered North America, many centuries before other European explorers.

Leonardo Da Vinci
(1452, Italy)

Made many inventions and discoveries in science and maths, and created lots of amazing artwork.

William Shakespeare
(1564, United Kingdom)

Wrote 37 incredible plays as well as over 150 poems, which are still studied, read and performed today.

**Isaac Newton
(1643, United Kingdom)**

Made many important discoveries in maths, physics and astronomy, including the discovery of gravity.

**Benjamin Franklin
(1706, British America)**

Fought for independence from Great Britain, as well as making many discoveries in electricity.

**Charles Babbage
(1791, United Kingdom)**

Engineered the first mechanical computer, which has inspired most modern technology we use today.

**Charles Darwin
(1809, United Kingdom)**

Sailed the world to study animal and plant life, before writing books on his theories of biology and evolution.

**Susan B. Anthony
(1820, United States)**

Played an important role in both the women's suffrage movement and abolitionism (the anti-slavery movement).

**Mohandas Gandhi
(1869, British India)**

Fought for independence from Great Britain, preaching nonviolence and inspiring other civil rights activists.

**Albert Einstein
(1879, Germany)**

Made many important theories and discoveries in physics and astronomy, including his theory of relativity.

**Edmund Hillary
(1919, New Zealand)**

Reached the highest point in the world, Mount Everest, Along with Tenzing Norgay, a Nepalese Sherpa.

**Martin Luther King, Jr.
(1929, United States)**

Became the leader of the civil rights movement, which aimed to give more rights and freedom to African Americans.

So there we have it, Zobb. Humans are a fascinating bunch of animals who have changed their world over thousands of years. They build, travel, discover, play, and do many, many, many other things.

They sometimes fight with one another, but in order to survive as a species, they must all learn to love themselves, each other, and the planet they live on.

Humans are weird.

...Yes, I suppose they are. Right, we'd better head off home now - we've got 10 billion kilometres of outer space to get through. Let's go, Zobb!

12393809R00020

Printed in Great Britain
by Amazon